D1393145

Beyond
Imagination

To Laura?

Victoria Ancona-Vincent

**Victoria
Ancona-Vincent**

WITNESS COLLECTION

Series editor: Stephen Smith

BEYOND IMAGINATION

By Victoria Ancona-Vincent

Published in Great Britain by
Beth Shalom Ltd.
Laxton, Newark,
Nottinghamshire NG22 0PA

British Library Cataloguing in Publication Data
A catalogue record for this book is available from the
British Library.

ISBN 1 900381 00 1

Printed and bound by Mallard Imaging, Kimberley,
Nottingham.

CONTENTS

Victoria Ancona - Vincent

Holocaust Survivor A-5346

EVERY story must be told.

IF ALL the experiences of those who suffered under the Nazi regime's hideous policies towards the Jews were to be written down, there would be more than we could read - it would be more than we could bear. Only a fraction of those who survived have been able to pass on their experiences, and those who perished have never been heard at all. It is often said that deportees in the camps vowed to speak and to bear witness to the atrocities which they saw and experienced. This series of survivor accounts is an attempt to ensure that the voices of these witnesses are heard.

THIS BOOK is about one woman's experience under the Nazi regime. She assisted in the Italian Resistance, was arrested by the Gestapo and held in the San Vittorio prison, Milan for 6 months and later deported to Auschwitz, where she spent eight months. Four traumatic months on death marches followed as she was moved from one camp to another, constantly on the point of death, before she was liberated by the Russian forces.

VICTORIA Ancona-Vincent has condensed her experiences into a short, but highly informative autobiographical account. Her attention to detail goes back to the period of her captivity, when she realised the importance of remembering things accurately. She kept a diary while she was in the Resistance, which was later confiscated by the Gestapo on her arrest. After being in Auschwitz, in the last days of the war, Victoria kept a piece of paper in her shoe, on which she wrote the dates of the most significant moments of her story. The result of this, combined with her vivid memory, is a concise yet accurately detailed record of her traumatic experiences.

VICTORIA'S account joins many hundreds of others, each as tragic, each as painful, as the horrors of the camps still unfold. It is to these people that we owe much of what we know and understand of the personal tragedy of the Nazi years. This series of Holocaust survivor testimonies has not been published to create literary masterpieces, but to tell and to tell again, that which needs to be heard and heard again.

Stephen D. Smith
Series Editor.

ACKNOWLEDGEMENTS

IT HAS taken many years for me even to contemplate writing my testimony, partly because I was afraid to relive what happened, and partly because I was concerned that I may not be understood or believed. Today I am pleased that my story can be told and I would therefore like to thank those who have assisted me.

I WOULD like to thank my husband Alfred Vincent who has not only been a loving, faithful and caring friend since we met in Milan in 1946, but who has encouraged me right through the writing of my testimony and has been tireless in his assistance and devotion. Without him it would simply not have been done.

I WOULD also like to thank my sister Olga, who understands everything. And Rachel who shares it all.

NATURALLY I am always grateful to my son David, who has been a wonderful son and has encouraged me to share my story, to his wife, Jill and my two dear grand children Sarah and Jonathan, who are such a wellspring of life in my older years.

FINALLY, I would like to thank Stephen and James Smith for being part of a younger generation prepared to listen and to help to keep the tragic memory of the Holocaust alive. Their eagerness to assist me to publish my testimony has been a tremendous source of encouragement to me, as it will doubtless be to others like me. Thank You.

To my son, David.

INTRODUCTION

IT HAS taken many years for me even to speak of my time in Auschwitz. But now, fifty years later, this is the testimony of my experiences before, during and after the Holocaust.

BEFORE THE Nazi invasion of Italy, I wrote five volumes of diaries in French between the 31st July 1937 and the 9th November 1943. These included some of the experiences which my family and I went through under the Italian racial laws against the Jews. The fifth and last volume of my diaries, in which I recorded my anti-Nazi feelings, was taken by the Gestapo on the day of my arrest. I never saw this volume again. The first four volumes were kept safely at the country cottage in Rovigo, owned by my employer and fellow Resistance worker, Miss Giovanna Fogagnolo, and given back to me after the war, on my return to Milan. The dates and events I have written about during the pre-war period were taken from my diaries. The dates recording my experiences at Auschwitz-Birkenau, Auschwitz I, the death marches and other camps, were written on a small piece of paper, still in my possession, which I kept in my shoe during the final days of the war.

MY TESTIMONY has been written to the best of my recollection. I have tried to ensure the accuracy of it by carefully checking dates and referring to documents of the period. I have kept my text concise and have avoided elaborate descriptive details. I hope through this, that the experiences I have written can be used for educational means in the studies of the Holocaust.

V.A.V.

JERUSALEM TO MILAN

Moments of
Happiness

Photo: Our house in Ruchama, Jerusalem

I WAS born in Jerusalem on the 26th June 1923 during the time of the British Mandate. I am the youngest of nine children, Lea, Marco (Mordecai), Moshe, Albert (Avraham), Allégra (Simhah), Edmond, Olga, Rachel and myself.

MY FATHER, Saul Mordecai Ancona, my mother, Nezhah Ancona, my brothers and sisters and some of my relatives, were born in Aleppo, Syria. My mother died when she was thirty-nine years old, shortly after my birth, although I was never told the cause of her death. Of my family today, only my sisters Olga and Rachel are still alive. My father was a banker and stockbroker and had moved to Jerusalem. We first lived in the Buchara district of Jerusalem and later, in a large stone house in Ruchama near Mahane Yehuda Street. I have many happy memories of that time although I was only six years old when we eventually left Jerusalem for Brussels.

TO ME as a child in 1929, the Arab uprising in Palestine was very frightening. Women and children were kept indoors, all the windows and some doors were barricaded. When Olga, Rachel and I eventually returned to school, the Alliance Israélite Universelle, we were taken by horse carriage, under escort.

AT THE end of 1929, my sister Lea was married to David. She had looked after me since our mother died, and I was very upset when I realised that she would no longer be living at home with us, but with her new husband. They eventually had four children, Tova, Hemda, Ezra and Ruth, who now live in Tel-Aviv. My sisters and I are in close contact with them.

MY FATHER, who had re-married a kind French woman, Esther Bijio, whom we called 'Aunt Esther', decided to transfer his business to Brussels. Before we left Jerusalem in May 1930, I understand that he donated our house for use as a Yeshivah, and as far as I know, it is still being used as such today. My brothers attended universities in Paris and Montpellier, and when we settled in Brussels, they worked in my father's business.

MY FATHER, stepmother, brother Albert and sisters Allégra, Rachel, Olga and I left by ship from Jaffa to Trieste. We arrived in Brussels and after a couple of months of living in a rented flat, we settled in our home in 12 Av. d'Auderghem. Olga, Rachel and I went to a French speaking school, 'Cours d'Education C.' in 68, rue de Gravelines. The only language we had spoken until then was Hebrew, but we quickly learnt French and soon spoke less and less Hebrew.

MY FATHER'S financial situation was very good and we lived surrounded by luxury. However, Olga, Rachel and I were kept at home with our stepmother, where we lived a very sheltered life. My father was a gentle and quiet man and would have given us anything we wanted, but we never really thought of asking. In 1933, we moved to a much larger house in 7 Square Ambiorix. My stepmother engaged two live-in maids to help her run the house.

IN THE summer of 1933, my sister Allégra was married. She lived in Brussels with her husband, Roger, but I missed her very much. She had watched over me since Lea was married. Allégra and Roger had two daughters, Yvette and Danielle, who have always lived in Brussels with their respective families. They are very close to my sisters and me.

WE CONTINUED to celebrate the Jewish festivals in Brussels as we had done in Jerusalem, although somehow it was not quite the same. At Pesach, the whole family including Allégra and Roger, gathered for the Seder. When we went back to school, we took Matzo for our mid-morning break. The Belgian girls were inquisitive, but I never felt the need to hide the fact that I was Jewish. Antisemitism was never a problem to us in Brussels. I made friends with some of the Belgian girls and to this day I still correspond with one of them.

IN 1935, my brothers Moshe and Albert went to settle in Tel-Aviv and began their own business there. A year later, Marco went to Buenos Aires to join some of our cousins there. My brother Edmond, who had read law at Montpellier University, joined us in Brussels in 1934. He was the youngest of my brothers, and my sisters and I were very attached to him. We were all very upset when in 1935, he fell ill and died shortly after. Out of nine children only three of us were now living with our father and stepmother—Olga, Rachel and myself.

IN 1936, my father transferred his business to Alexandria, Egypt. Rachel and I went to a boarding school in Brussels for one year before rejoining the family in July 1937 in Alexandria. We moved into a house on a street appropriately named Rue des Pharaons and I went to the English College for Girls. Rachel continued her studies in music and ballet. I do not remember much about our short stay in Alexandria. However, I do recall that we stayed in a nice area of the city and would love to ride to school on the bus each day, watching the coastline along La Corniche, a beautiful wide promenade flanked with cafés. As far as I understand it, the business in Alexandria was not a success, and so in December 1937, my father returned to Europe via Italy. Two months later, we rejoined him in Milan where my father had provisionally rented a flat in 7 via Visconti Venosta. He immediately applied for the family to be included in the USA Italian Immigration Quota. His intention was to take us to New York to join two of his brothers and one sister who lived there.

BY THE summer of 1938, we had not received any notification for our names to be included in the USA Italian Immigration Quota and we never did. When we tried to renew them, our passports had been confiscated by the authorities and we were forced to remain in Italy. I went to a French school until July 1938, when Italy proclaimed racial laws forbidding Jews from attending non-Jewish schools. So I went to a Jewish school until June 1939, when the Italian fascist government closed all Jewish schools, thus curtailing the education of Jews. The racial laws in Italy closed around us like a net. One bad regulation led to another until we found ourselves without the possibility of education or work and no form of income.

MY FATHER had not been permitted to start any new business and was very concerned about his financial position. Jews could only find employment as undeclared employees and were paid much less than the normal rate. My father was unable to find any employment. In June 1939, he tried again to arrange for me to leave Italy and go to either Tel-Aviv or Jerusalem as I had been born in Jerusalem during the British Mandate. But the Palestine regulation was that I required two years subsistence money. This was out of the question. We had gone from being comfortably well-off to being without any means of supporting ourselves in a matter of a couple of years.

On 1st September 1939, Olga was accepted by the Berlitz school of languages in Trieste, as a teacher of French and English. Rachel, who had trained as a ballet dancer, found undeclared employment in a ballet touring company. I gave some private French lessons to children and adults. Individually the Italians were sympathetic towards the Jews, even though they were at risk with the authorities for employing them. New restrictions were brought in against Jews in the September of 1939. They had to have new identity cards which carried the word 'Jew' and the owner's thumb print. Since we were law-abiding citizens, we dutifully complied with every restriction placed upon us.

IN NOVEMBER 1939, my father's financial situation had deteriorated yet further, and to meet expenses of rent and food, he sold most of the family's jewellery. By April 1940, our financial situation was becoming serious, and my father sold some of our furniture and our carpets to pay for one year's rent in advance for the one bedroom flat to which we were moving at 154, via Ripamonti.

ON THE 19th March 1940 I was not yet seventeen. I was so angry at not finding work, and always being hungry that, without telling anyone, I wrote a letter to Mussolini in Italian, which translates :

"Dear Sir,
Perhaps you do not realise that because Jews are not allowed to work, they are going hungry. Jews are also made of flesh and blood. I am sure you will find it in the kindness of your heart to revoke the racial laws. I thank you in advance."

AS A result of my letter, I received a written notification to report in person on the 3rd May 1940 to the Police headquarters in Milan. Having waited for over two hours, I was called into the office of the Chief of Police. I was informed that *'il Duce'* had received my letter, and his reply was that there was nothing he could do to help the Jews. I was very pleased to leave the police headquarters and to return home.

AT THE beginning of 1940, the Italian government set up labour legions for all the foreign born Jews. Because we were included in this category, my sisters and I received a written directive in June 1940, to report to a box making factory near Monza, one hour's journey by two trams from our house in Milan. There were about twenty of us Jewish girls. To us, the conditions seemed primitive as, of course, we had never worked in a factory. Our pay was lower than that of the regular Italian workers, and by comparison to them, we were considered too slow and unsuitable. As a result the Jewish workers were dismissed after only six weeks and replaced by Italians. Olga returned to her position at the Berlitz school. Rachel could not immediately rejoin the ballet touring company and found temporary employment with the Olivetti family in Ivrea, Piedmont, looking after their children. Every month, my sisters sent to my father whatever money they could afford to help us live.

AT THE end of July 1940, I found work in a typing agency, but my pay was very low. Mr Andreoli, a customer of the typing agency, wanted to engage a typist who could speak French, for his wholesale fruit business in Bressanone. I told him he would have to speak with my father, if he was offering me the job. He agreed and on the 2nd September 1940 he came to discuss the matter with my father. It was agreed that I would go to Bressanone, between Bolzano and the Brenner pass - about 300 km from Milan - on one month's trial, and that my pay would be 200 lire per month plus accommodation at a hotel, and my train fare to Bressanone. I left Milan on the 22nd September 1940 and started work on the following day. There was so little work, business must have been bad. I spent most of my time writing my diary and letters home. On the 2nd October 1940, I received a letter from my father telling me that Mr Andreoli's cheque for 200 lire, to pay for my train fare and part of my earnings, which I had given to my father, had bounced. My father had to pay 30 lire in stamp duty - enough for two days food for my father and stepmother. Mr Andreoli regretted this and gave me 250 lire to be sent to my father by postal order. I was already suspicious about my job, because there was so little work for me to do and I hardly ever saw any customers. I stayed at the Golden Cross hotel until the 17th October 1940, when Mr Andreoli said I would have to leave the hotel and sleep in an attic bedroom above the office. A few days later, the owner of the building came to the office and demanded his rent. On the 25th October 1940, two policemen came to the office and arrested Mr Andreoli. I was not sure why, but I suspected he had debts. I was called to the court as a witness. The magistrate accepted I knew nothing and was not involved in Mr Andreoli's dubious activities. Since he had not paid my wages in full and I had no money, the court supplied me with a rail warrant to return to Milan on Sunday the 29th of October 1940. The train in which I travelled was full of German military. I was thankful to reach Milan without incident and to be back with my family.

ON MY return home, once again I looked for work, but did not find any until 6th December 1940, when I began working in a bookshop in Corso di Porta Vittoria. At the bookshop, there was always a quarrelsome atmosphere between the owner and his wife. On 8th October 1941, I took a day off and looked for other employment. I was accompanied by Rachel and she suggested that I enquire at Cappelli Publishers in Via Francesco Sforza. I was interviewed by a man named Franco Maisano. He was pleased that I had experience working in a book shop and that I could speak English and French. He said he did not have a vacancy but he thought he might be able to help me. In giving me back my identity card, which was stamped the word 'Jewish,' he said, "it's all right, do not worry." He quickly wrote a quick note and gave it to me addressed to Miss

Giovanna Fogagnolo, 40 Corso Venezia. He told me to go there the following evening, after six o'clock. The following day I went to the book shop and I met Miss Fogagnolo and gave her the envelope from Mr Maisano. After a little while, he came into the shop and they both went into a back room. They soon came out and offered me undeclared employment to start work on the 15th October 1941. They seemed very pleased I could speak English. Both were very nice to me and they told me that I would have a position of trust and would be the only employee.

FROM THE end of 1941, Milan was regularly bombed and we spent many nights seeking shelter in the cellars. Often we would have to walk to and from work as the tram system was out of action because of the debris all over the city.

AFTER TWO months, I was given a key to the premises, because Miss Fogagnolo often came late and sometimes left early. At times, Miss Fogagnolo would hand me a book or two, in which she had already inserted a sealed envelope and asked me to make a parcel, for me to deliver by hand. She instructed me that if the person to whom the parcel was addressed was not there, to bring it back.

OCCASIONALLY, I noticed that there were large sums of money in the cash box, far in excess of the previous day's takings. I became concerned and I mentioned this to Miss Fogagnolo, who told me not to worry; she would deal with the money.....

CHAPTER TWO

RESISTANCE

Confronting
my Enemy

Photo: Victoria aged 17, whilst in the Resistance

I CONTINUED to work in the shop for Giovanna Fogagnolo throughout the winter. Very often, unfamiliar men would come to the shop to speak with Miss Fogagnolo. Sometimes the strange visitors were women.

I BECAME more curious about the parcels, the visits and the money. When Miss Fogagnolo realised this, she came to speak to me and told me that she and her fiancé, Mr Maisano, were helping certain persons to avoid arrest. They knew I was Jewish, and were always friendly towards me, and so I asked if they were helping Jews to reach Switzerland. She replied that she and Mr. Maisano were in the Resistance and that Jews were being helped. "And you also," she said, "have been helping the Resistance. The parcels you have been delivering to various addresses contained hidden messages for the Resistance and we hope you will continue to help us in this way." I was only too pleased to help and readily accepted the risks involved.

I WAS eighteen years old, but possibly owing to insufficient food for the past three years, I had not developed physically and looked only fifteen years old.

Perhaps I also had the right innocent appearance for a Resistance messenger.

WE HAD now been without our radio for over a year. It had been confiscated by the Italian police on 15th January 1941. This made us feel even more isolated as we missed listening to the news from London and Paris. We had always looked forward so much to hearing the plays and concerts on the radio.

OUR SITUATION at home was getting desperate. We existed on my small wages plus whatever money Olga and Rachel could afford to send, whenever they worked. But when the rent was due, we really had a problem. There was nothing more my father could sell. He was forced to ask the Jewish community for help. This was very painful for him because hitherto he had always given large donations to the Jewish communities.

ITALIAN MONTHLY food rationing was minimal, not enough to live on. The vast majority of Italians who were working, were able to buy some food on the black market. We could not afford to do this. My stepmother was reduced to collecting discarded vegetables on her daily visits to the market, to supplement our pasta or rice meals. These were terrible and humiliating times for Jews. At meal times, my father would often say that he was not hungry and that he did not need the food because he was not working. My stepmother would insist on giving me her small portion, which I always refused, saying I had already eaten some food at the book shop. Each day I had to persuade my stepmother to serve equal portions and to encourage my father to eat.

RACHEL CAME home in between the engagements of the ballet touring company. Sometimes Olga was able to come home at the same time. We very much looked forward to seeing them; my father was so happy to have his three daughters with him. By this time I had been working at Miss Fogagnolo's book shop for over a year and a half, and was still delivering messages for the Resistance.

WITH THE fall of the fascist government, Mussolini was arrested on the 25th July 1943, and imprisoned in the Gran Sasso, Abruzzi. To most Italians, and above all to the Jews, it was as if a dark cloud had been lifted from over our heads. All of a sudden, there were no fascist black shirts to be seen and people started smiling and talking to each other, without any fear of being overheard. The atmosphere was euphoric. During the period of Mussolini's imprisonment, a few allied prisoners of war and some Italian antifascists escaped from captivity.

ON 10th September 1943, Mussolini was rescued by the Germans who were now occupying the Northern half of Italy. The Germans put Mussolini in charge of a puppet government, "la repubblica di Salò" in Lombardy, on Lake Garda. From the time of Mussolini's arrest, the bookshop had been used by the Italian Resistance to give overnight shelter, food and clothing to Allied Prisoners of War, and to help them reach Switzerland. When necessary, I was called upon as an interpreter. I was the person who opened the premises in the morning and I had to ensure there was no evidence of allied prisoners of war having stayed overnight.

AT NINE o'clock on the morning of 9th November 1943, two Germans in civilian clothing, whom I suspected were Gestapo, entered the bookshop and asked for Miss Fogagnolo. I explained she had not arrived. They said they would be back and then left. I was unable to locate Miss Fogagnolo in order to warn her, and she arrived shortly after ten o'clock, followed by the two Germans, who indeed were Gestapo. They took our identity cards, together with the fifth volume of my diary, in which I had recorded my family's day to day suffering under Italian racial laws, and my anti-nazi feelings. I never saw this volume of my diary again. After the war, I retrieved the remaining four volumes which had been hidden at Miss Fogagnolo's country cottage in Rovigo.

WITHOUT ANY questioning, the Gestapo arrested us both and took us to San Vittore prison, Milan. On arrival, we were taken to a courtyard where other men and women were standing with their hands up on the wall. We were forced to join them and stand, for three to four hours, with our hands up on the wall. The Germans fired shots above our heads. We were finally taken in for registration, then to the political section and locked in cells, two or three women per cell. My cell on Section III which I shared with Alba Zanfini, another resistance worker, was No.81. My prison number was No.537.

WE WOMEN had meals in a large room where we were allowed to stay for about two hours. After about ten days, during one of the meal sessions, Miss Fogagnolo became ill with abdominal pains and an hour or so later, the wardens took her away. We heard that she had been taken to hospital in Milan. I never saw her in San Vittore prison again. It emerged after the war that she had feigned appendicitis to obtain a place in the hospital, from where she was able to organise a place for herself in a mental asylum for the rest of the war. Miss Fogagnolo knew how to escape trouble!

I WAS very worried about my family, who knew nothing about my work with the Italian Resistance. After the war, I learned that on the day of my arrest, the Gestapo searched our flat on 154 via Ripamonti, Milan, looking for anything connecting me to the Resistance. They did not arrest my family, who immediately went into hiding in Ferrara with friends of my sister Rachel. These non-Jewish friends sheltered my father, my stepmother and Rachel until the end of the war. In order to get a new identity, my family told the Ferrara authorities that their name was Marconi, that they came from Pesaro, which had been heavily bombed, and that they had lost most of their belongings and identity cards. They were issued with identity and ration cards bearing their new name, without the thumb print or the word 'Jewish'. Rachel was fortunate enough to find employment in the Registry Office.

IN SAN Vittore prison, a British prisoner of War named Jim, was used by the Germans as interpreter, both at the registration stage and also around the prison. He was very kind and said he would try hide my papers in order to delay the date of my interrogation. Whatever he did worked as I was not interrogated for six months.

AT THE beginning of January 1944, I fell ill with pneumonia. My cellmate, Alba Zanfini, looked after me. An Italian warder put a little stove in the cell which had been terribly cold. I was given nothing to relieve my illness and it lasted the whole of January and a good part of February. On 17th February 1944, we were transferred to the women's section, which was kept by the nuns, who acted both as prison wardens and guardians in the frequent bombing raids.

BECAUSE OF my weakened condition after suffering pneumonia, my fellow prisoners became concerned for my health. A friend of mine, Elena Banfi, who also worked for the Resistance, was the daughter of a doctor of medicine, and as a non-Jew, was allowed clothing parcels from home. She was able to get for me some vials of calcium, with which the nuns injected me. I do not know whether it improved my condition, but the gesture meant a lot at the time.

AT THE end of April 1944 my turn for interrogation by the Gestapo eventually came. Unnecessary and irrelevant questions were repeated over and over again, as were the slaps and beatings. I do not know what they sought to achieve, as my fate had already been decided simply by virtue of my racial status. After the brutal interrogation, I was moved from the political to the Jewish section of the prison, on 3rd May 1944. On the evening of 15th May 1944, I was transported with all the Jews in the section to Fossoli transit camp near Modena. Until September 1943, Fossoli camp had been used as a camp for British prisoners of war - now it served a more sinister purpose.

CHAPTER THREE

AUSCHWITZ - BIRKENAU

Inside the Inferno

Photo: Main gate at Auschwitz - Birkenau

THE NEXT evening, 16th May 1944, about five hundred and seventy five men, women and children, were marched to the railway siding at the edge of Fossoli camp and loaded into cattle wagons by SS guards. We were given a small piece of bread and a bucket of water to be shared amongst one hundred of us. Nothing else. The wagon doors were sealed and the train set off. We had no idea where we were going. We were so cramped in the wagon that we had to take it in turns to sit with our legs stretched out. All that was provided was a metal drum for us to relieve ourselves in front of each other. It was humiliating in the extreme.

AT LEAST three people died during the journey in our carriage. We nearly suffocated from the stench and the lack of air. We had to take it in turns to breathe fresh air from the small grilles, near the top of the wagon, climbing over each other's legs. Our train was destined for Auschwitz-Birkenau and during the terrible, six-day journey from Fossoli, the doors were only opened once for us to empty the latrine drums. We were given another bucket of water, but no food. The SS did not take the dead out of the wagons.

WE ARRIVED at Birkenau in the evening of the 22nd May 1944, but we were left in the sealed wagons until the morning of 23rd May 1944. The doors were opened by men in striped clothing, and SS guards with barking dogs herded us out of the wagons shouting *'Raus! Raus! Schnell! Schnell!'*. We were instructed to take only our hand luggage. I did not know where we were, nor did I know what was really going on there. As we had been waiting in the wagons the night before, we had been aware of the very strong odour of burning flesh, but could not understand what it was. We certainly did not even consider that they might be burning people. What we were about to encounter was beyond imagination.

I WAS at Auschwitz, but I felt no fear there. The only thing which troubled me on my arrival were the ferocious dogs, which I hoped would not be allowed to bite. After climbing out of the wagon on to the ramp, we were separated from the men, and arranged in rows of five. The unloading ramp stretched the length of the camp and all I could see was a mass of people in front and behind me. Although the SS were hurrying the process along, there was no real commotion or panic, other than distressed children who wandered around

looking for their fathers or crying for their mothers.
Slowly the column moved forward until I found myself
standing in front of a small wooden desk. I was later to
discover that SS officer with the white gloves
conducting the selection that day, was the notorious Dr
Mengele, who, with the move of his finger indicated
left towards death and right to live a little while longer.
He calmly sent the old, the infirm, the sick, the women
with children, the pregnant women, the young women
who would not leave their mothers or older relations,
all to the left side. The few of us who remained were
marched away. We presumed that the other group were
being taken to a special camp, because it was clear that
they were less able-bodied than the group I was with.
Of the five hundred and seventy five on the transport,
only fifty-seven were not sent straight to the gas
chambers.

WE WERE taken to a low brick building known as the
sauna and ordered to undress. Our bodies were searched
by male deportees. Every piece of jewellery was taken
from us. We were then pushed into the shower room
and when we came out, our belongings and clothing
were gone. Next, other male deportees shaved our

heads, armpits and between our legs. I felt very ashamed. After waiting what seemed to be hours, we were given our 'new' clothes! I was given ill fitting wooden clogs and a dirty looking rough dress, covered with insect marks. The dress had a two inch stripe of red paint along its back. We were then ordered to go into another room, where female deportees were sitting at small tables. There were queues at each table. When my turn came, the girl asked my name, my age and where I came from, and entered the details in what looked like a register. She then tattooed my left forearm with the number A-5346 - my new identity.

WE WERE marched, in ranks of five, to the quarantine section of the camp, where I was to spend the next two months. As we walked, we asked each other in a very low voice, what the horrid stench was which we had smelled on arrival, and could still smell wherever we went. We saw flames coming out of a very tall chimney, not far from the 'sauna'. It was not long before we knew the horrifying truth. Jews were being gassed and burned here.

OUR BLOCK housed about one thousand deportees.

In charge of the block were a *'blocova'* and a *'stubova'*. They were either Polish, German or Eastern European - all non-Jews. They were responsible for the discipline of the block, and enjoyed their superior position, especially because they were able to get extra food. They were very strong and as brutal as the SS, particularly with new deportees.

IN THE block, there were three tier bunks, each covered with a thin palliasse and a blanket. Ten women slept head to foot on each one. The SS were fanatic about bed making. We were punished if the palliasses were not completely flattened and the blankets not tucked in, with corners at each end, in the shape of a flat box. We were given a reddish brown enamel tin bowl, which we kept tied around our waist, day and night. Without it, we would not be given soup or the brownish watery liquid they called coffee.

OUR DAILY routine was one of hunger, exhaustion and fear. We were awakened at three or four in the morning and had to stand outside in silence, whatever the weather, in rows of five, in front of the block for over three hours until everyone in the camp was counted by the SS. This was known as the roll call - *appell*. We were not even allowed to go to the latrines and since we suffered from persistent diarrhoea, we could not help but relieve ourselves on the spot. For this we were brutally beaten and punished. There were many types of punishment devised by the SS in Birkenau apart from the beatings. One was to stand outside the block all night, or to kneel on the muddy ground holding a brick in each hand for hours, or to run around the block until you were told to stop. Running with clogs which sunk into the deep mud and made them heavier was almost impossible for our weakened bodies.

AFTER ROLL call, we were given weak, tepid liquid which was called 'coffee'. Nothing else. For most of the day, we had to wait, at the back of the block, to be detailed for work in the camp. The duties could be anything, but was often putting deportees who had died on the wooden stretchers - *tragen* - and carrying these to an area indicated by the kapos. The kapos were mainly German common criminals who wore a green triangle on their blue and white striped jacket. The SS put the kapos in charge of our work details, which included emptying the latrines into barrels, then lifting the barrels on to carts and pushing the carts over the muddy ground to cesspits outside the camp; on the other hand we could be made to carry the heavy soup drums from the kitchens to the block. Whatever way you could be used to do the menial, dehumanising and dirty work, the SS and kapos would ensure that you did it.

EVERY ORDER the SS, the Kapos and the blocovas shouted at us was in German. Orders had to be carried out in double time. This made life more difficult for those of us who did not know the language. Because we did not understand the orders, we were dealt more blows, with whips or clubs, on our heads and bodies. As we grew weaker, one blow was sufficient to knock us to the ground.

THE SS, the kapos and the blocovas seemed to compete with each other in the bestial treatment of the Jews. In addition to the brutality of the SS towards us, we had to suffer the threatening behaviour of the other non-Jewish Germans, Poles and Ukrainians. They tried to steal our bread rations, and our soup bowls, whether full or empty. Obtaining by stealing, finding, bartering, and any other means was called 'organising' in the camp.

IN THE middle of the day, we were given soup. Nothing else. This contained bromide and was foul. There were potato peelings and the occasional cabbage leaf or small piece of swede, which was a luxury. Often we would fish out the odd button, nail and floating insects. For the first two or three days, few of us could bring ourselves to touch the soup. Women had added concerns when their menstruation stopped. We thought it must be due to starvation and the bromide the SS put in the soup.

AFTER AFTERNOON roll call, which lasted two hours, we were given a small chunk of nearly black and very dry bread with either a tiny round piece of rancid margarine or a blob of sugar beet jam or a thin, small round slice of something resembling salami. Nothing to drink. Thirst and dehydration was a constant agony. Any water would have been good, but the other deportees, who had been longer in the camp, warned us that it was dangerous to drink water in the camp's washroom.

I HAD been in Birkenau for about a week when one morning, after roll call, the SS asked if any deportees had two sets of grandparents of the same nationality. Some of the women raised their hand. They were taken away. We learnt later that they had been taken to the experiments block. We never saw them again.

ON THE evening of 15th June 1944, some girls from our block were waiting to go in for our first shower in the camp - without soap or towel. As we waited, I saw a group of women deportees approaching with SS guards. The girls were talking with each other and I thought I heard my sister's voice. "Olga?", I said to myself, "Here? not possible." I waited until the group came nearer and I shouted her name in disbelief. I wanted so much to be wrong. I was shocked when she actually turned round and looked at me. We recognised each other, as difficult as it was, in such circumstances. It was painful for both of us to know that the other was also in Birkenau. We did not have time to touch hands and only managed to say a few words. We wanted to embrace but it would have been dangerous to attract the attention of the SS. Neither of us cried, but we were deeply saddened to meet in this terrifying place. Olga's number is 76785, with a small triangle underneath the number.

OCCASIONALLY, when my sister's group returned in the evening from their work at the *Schuhkommando,* she would try to see and to speak to me. One day she gave me a clove of garlic which she had 'organised' - it was my twenty-first birthday. During the time I was in quarantine, my face and body became covered with red spots. On 29th July 1944, there was a medical inspection of the block. What we feared was that it might be a selection? Fortunately it was not, and I was taken with other girls to the infirmary *-revier -* because I had measles. I feared the worst for myself, as I had heard very few people survived the infirmary, mainly because of the selections which took place there.

IN THE infirmary, there was a lady doctor and her assistants, all deportees. There were three tier narrow bunks, two deportees to each bunk, one blanket between two. There must have been a recent selection, because the infirmary was almost empty. We received no medication and surprisingly, we did not have to work. We still had to stand outside in front of the infirmary at roll calls, and wait until the SS had counted everyone in the camp. There was little the Jewish doctor could do to help us, other than be sympathetic.

ON 14th August 1944, I was very relieved to be discharged from the infirmary and surprised to be immediately transferred to the working camp, where I joined my sister at the *'Schuhkommando'*. I learned later that Olga had given several of her bread rations to the blocova, so that I would be with her in block 11. I was so pleased that my sister also 'organised' a size 3 pair of boots for me, because the clogs I had been given were far too large for me and cut into my feet. I knew this meant that Olga must have given up more of her bread ration to help me.

AFTER MORNING roll call, we went to the washrooms and tried to keep clean, with water only. We left the camp for work which was about sixty minutes walking distance. Then without any food, we had to line up in columns of five per row, stand straight like soldiers, and only when the SS guards were satisfied did they give the order to march. Anyone out of line would be beaten, punished or threatened to be sent to the crematorium.

Our house in Brussels -
Belgium, until 1936.

Olga, Rachael and I at Lake
Como in 1946.

My Father and I at
Milan Cathedral in 1946.

Alfred and I in Sempione Park
Milan - Nov 1946.

Olga.

Miss Fogagnolo, my "Employer"
and collaborator in the Resistance
- Milan, Jan 1943.

Olga and Rachael, Wollaton Park, Nottingham.

My son David in Nottingham - 1948.

Alfred and I.

Olga with my grandaughter - Sarah in 1989.

David.

A. P. P. I. A.
(ASSOCIAZIONE NAZIONALE PERSEGUITATI
—— POLITICI ITALIANI ANTIFASCISTI) ——

Tessera provvisoria N°   278

del Socio *Ancona*

Vittoria

di *Saulle*

e di *Mirra Ancona*

nato a *Gerusalemme*

il *23-6-1923*

domiciliato a *Milano*

Data *1-11-945*

IL PRESIDENTE

My Italian Antifascist
Members card - 1945.

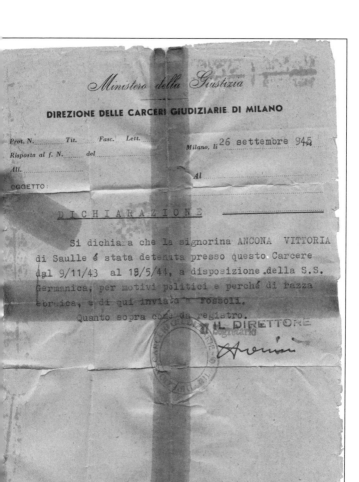

cument given to me by San Vittore prison confirming
status as an ex prisoner under the SS.
eads:

> *"We declare that Miss Victoria Ancona, daughter of Saul, has been detained in this prison,
> from the 9th November 1943 to the 15th May 1944, at the disposal of the German SS, for
> political motives and for being Jewish, and from here sent to Fossoli.*
> *The above as per register.*
> *The Director."*

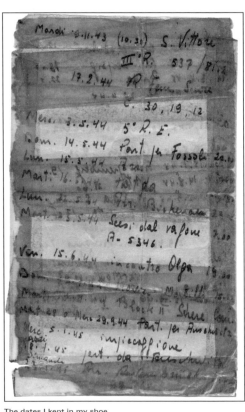

The dates I kept in my shoe
during the last days of the War.

CENTRO ASSISTENZA REDUCI GERMANIA | C.L.N.M. | U.D.I.

TESSERA DI RICONOSCIMENTO N. 49859

POLITICO

EF
COGNOME E NOME ANCONA VITTORIA

PATERNITÀ SAULLE NATO A GERUSALEMME IL 23.6.23

STATO CIVILE: NUBILE PROFESSIONE STUDENTE

DOMICILIATO A MILANO VIA RIPAMONTI 154 N.

ARRIVATO A MILANO IL 12.9 BAGNO IL 12.9.45

VISITA MEDICA IL 12.9.45 DIRETTO A

DOCUMENTO IDENTITÀ SCHEDA RIMPATRIO RILASCIATO A BOLZANO

FIRMA DELL'ASSISTITO

Ancona Vittoria

LAGOMARSINO - SCHEDARI COMPONIBILI - 145X105

DATA 12.9 1945
L'UFFICIO EMITTENTE

AUSWITZ

MOD. CMP 2355
50.000 - 6.45

entity card which helped my
patriation. It also confirms my
atus as an Auschwitz Survivor.

NEAR THE camp gate, an orchestra of women deportees was forced to play mainly marches.. They were there in the morning and again in the evening, when we returned from work. We had to march in step, guarded by the SS and their vicious dogs and sing German songs. If we were out of step, stopped walking or did not sing, we were beaten with clubs or whips on the head. Because I was very short-sighted, Olga and I were always very concerned for the safety of my spectacles, since without them I could hardly see where I was going. I certainly could not see to work. It would have been the end for me.

AT THE *Schuhkommando*, we had to strip the mouldy and rusty shoes and boots of the deportees with a small sharp tool. Whenever we came across a child's shoes, we were saddened beyond words because we knew what happened to everyone here. But the children.... it was beyond thinking of.

IN THE hut where we worked, there were about thirty long benches. We sat on stools and in front of us, on the benches, were several boxes in which we had to place separately, the tops, the soles, the heels, the laces and the buttons. In another hut nearby were stored many thousands of boots, shoes and sandals which had belonged to all the deportees who had been brought to Birkenau, dead or alive. The shoes for stripping were fetched in sacks and everytime a sack was emptied, the smell and the large cloud of dust which covered us, made us cough.

A FRIENDSHIP had begun in the *Schuhkommando* between ten of us; one Italian, Giuliana Tedeschi from Turin, seven French girls, Julianne Hechter from Paris, Berthe, whom we called 'Tante Berthe' because she was already in her forties, Violette, Therese, Huguette, two other girls whose names I cannot recall, my sister and me.

I REMEMBER one occasion when two or three hundred of us were taken to the disinfecting block. Our clothes were put in large vats. We had to wait for hours before we were given back our clothes. They were not the same ones we had before, but as before, some fitted, most did not.

THROUGHOUT the months we were in Birkenau, the

selections for the gas chambers were carried out at any time and regardless of the weather. We were forced to stand naked outside and wait for hours for Dr Mengele and other SS. When our turn came we tried to stop shivering, stand very straight and look strong. It was beyond any human understanding, why some of us were deemed fit to work and others to die.

TO BE together was a great comfort for my sister and me, but we also had a constant worry for each other. In addition to the selections, there was a considerable number of deaths from typhus, cholera, dysentery, beatings and starvation. Apart from the selections for the gas chambers and disease, we were also at great risk of being chosen for 'medical' experiments by Dr Mengele and his staff at Auschwitz I. Many women went insane and were taken away, and we never saw them again; others tried to commit suicide on the high voltage electric perimeter fence. In most cases, the poor women could not even put an end to their own lives because the SS guards from the watchtowers shot them before they could reach the fence. If it was dark, the SS would pick them out with their searchlights.

WE CONSTANTLY suffered from subcutaneous eruptions all over our bodies, because of the lack of vitamins. The skin opened and pus ran out. We tried to hide any signs of illness from the SS as we knew only too well what would happen to us. The sight of the flames coming out of the tall chimney of the crematorium and the stench of burning flesh in our nostrils never allowed us to forget.

WHEN WE were in the camps, we were always worried about our families, so whenever there was a train of deportees from Italy, my sister and I asked if there were any 'Ancona' on the train. A negative answer provided only temporary relief.

FROM THE day of our arrival to the day we left Birkenau, trainloads of deportees continued to arrive night and day, from many countries in Europe. In the summer of 1944, there were many trains from Hungary. The Hungarian Jews who came to the camps were a very sad sight. They kept looking and asking for other Hungarians. They could not believe their families and friends who had not come into the work camp had been selected to die on arrival. We felt very sorry for them.

TO SURVIVE one more hour, one more day, you had to eat the foul food, to sleep the hours you could, to be alert and only work when you were watched, to obey every order quickly, to give no reason to the SS, the kapos, the blocovas to beat you—in any case you would be beaten enough—to be unnoticeable, above all, to believe with all your might that you would come out of this hell. We had to resist by all possible means the Nazi's aim of annihilating us.

ON 29th September 1944, we were transferred from Auschwitz-Birkenau extermination camp to the main Auschwitz camp which was about one hour's walking distance from Birkenau. We were housed in brick buildings, but otherwise there was no difference in the SS brutal treatment towards us.

AFTER A while, we finished at the *Schuhkommando* and were made to move either paving stones, bucketfuls of broken stones, or long heavy planks of wood from one place to another. The following day we had to move them back again. This useless task was one of the many ways by which the SS tried to dehumanise us. But we knew that if we did not resist their attempts, we would not survive. We felt we had to survive and tell what happened and what we saw in Auschwitz-Birkenau. We promised each other that we would tell.

LATER WE were taken to the sand quarry to dig out sand with picks and shovels, put it in barrows, and take the barrows to the small rail wagons. As the months went by it became bitterly cold with icy winds. Some of us were clothed in only a thin dress and we had no cover on our shaven heads. The leaden sky, the biting cold weather, the screeching of the crows, the shouting, insulting SS and the barking of their dogs made our existence even worse in these wintry conditions. We were growing weaker and weaker. The heavy work of moving stones, planks and sand was becoming too much for our debilitated bodies. One of our group would always be on the lookout, and when the SS were furthest away from us, we rested on our shovels. Our group of ten friends tried to stay together and we never allowed ourselves to feel nostalgic. We never cried. We never said 'if we get back home' but 'when'. We spoke of composers and authors and tried to remember bars of music and titles of books. There were many groups of women friends like ours throughout the camp. They showed the same resistance and determination to survive. We knew that those who could not accept the terrible conditions, those who did not eat, did not work, those who let their feelings overtake them, would quickly become *'muselmänner'* - a term used in the camp to indicate those who had given up the fight for survival - and would soon be selected for the gas chambers.

ON THE 5th of January 1945, four girls who worked in the Union explosives factory, were accused of sabotage by supplying gunpowder for the blowing up of one of the crematoria in early October 1944. On returning from the sand quarry, we were forced to stand, with the other deportees and watch with open eyes the hanging of two of the girls. One of the girls' sister, who stood nearby, was crying and the SS woman guard shouted at her to stop crying, if not, she would send her to join them. It was a horrifying scene which my sister and I can never forget. The hanging of the other two girls was carried out the following morning, for the returning night shift workers to witness. Two weeks before, the SS had put up a Christmas tree. It was still there when they built the scaffold nearby and carried out the hangings of the four girls.

CHAPTER FOUR

DEATH MARCHES

Beyond the Gates of Hell

VERY EARLY in the morning of the 18th January 1945, the SS evacuated Auschwitz camp in a hurry because of the Russian advance. We were told to take a blanket, but were given no food or drink. It was freezing cold. The death march had begun.

AFTER ABOUT two hours marching, we came across a cartload of bread. It had turned on its side, in the ditch and was covered with snow. The bread was white in the usual loaf shape, the likes of which we had not seen or tasted for a long time. The deportees nearest to the cart ignored the SS and rushed to get some of the bread. One of our group of ten friends managed to get part of a loaf which we shared between us. The whole incident was over in a few minutes. The SS threatened to shoot us if we did not get back into the column.

THE DEPORTEES who stepped out of line, stopped or did not keep up with the long column, were shot dead. We had to step over the dead and the dying as we marched. To our horror, Violette, one of our group had strayed behind, and we heard she had been shot dead. We were made to walk continuously. The SS men and women were changed every four hours. They wore warm clothing and boots. We had thin dresses and one small blanket, and not everyone had head covering.

AT THIS time, surprisingly and inconveniently, my menstruation started again, for this month's cycle only. It did not return again until December 1945. It was difficult and painful to walk. The skin on my thighs had broken and the blood was drying on the open wounds. I tore strips from my dress and Olga and I gathered snow to wash the wounds and cool my thighs. I had to keep up with the column.

IN THE evening of the first day, the SS stopped the column. We were told to go down a long sloping bank to a large field, where we spent the night sleeping on the grass, in the snow. We were given a small chunk of black bread and a small piece of margarine. I used all my margarine and some of my sister's as an ointment to soothe my thighs.

THE SECOND day, the 19th Jan. 1945, was still bitterly cold. It continued to snow. We were very thirsty but were given nothing to drink. We tried to collect clean snow to quench our thirst. We had been walking since very early morning and we passed through some villages. At one of these small villages, some women came out of their houses. Having seen the column, they went back in and came out again with jugs full of water. The SS kept pushing them back with rifle butts. Only a few deportees managed to get a drink. We walked all day with short halts, without any food or drink. At intervals, throughout the second day, we heard rifle or revolver shots and we knew that more deportees were being shot dead by the SS. In the evening we were given a smaller piece of bread with a tiny round of margarine; again I used it to soothe the wounds on my thighs. On the second night a few deportees, including our group of now nine friends, slept in a cow shed. I do not know where the rest of the column slept.

ON THE third day, the 20th Jan. 1945, the death march started at dawn. After two to three hours, we came to the outskirts of a small town, which looked deserted. At an intersection, there was a corner building with an entry on the front. As we drew level with the entrance, Thérèse, the most lively of our group, who knew German, Polish and French, suddenly dashed out of the column and disappeared into a building in a matter of seconds.

I never knew what happened to her, but I very much hope she survived. Our group of ten friends was now down to eight.

THE DEATH march continued.

THE RIFLE shots had increased so much, that each shot sounded like an echo of the previous one. By now we were very tired and so weak that we were sleeping while we were marching. We marched like automatons. It became dark early and we kept calling each other's names to make sure we were still together, to keep ourselves awake and to prevent each other from falling. We spent the third night in the open, in the freezing cold and snow. We blew on each others back for a feeling of warmth.

ON THE fourth day, the 21st Jan. 1945, we were taken to a train and pushed into open wagons. There were about seventy deportees in each wagon and one SS armed guard. It snowed most of the time and the wind was icy cold. We were very cramped. A Polish girl, much stronger and bigger than I was, wanted more room. She began insulting Jews and then started pushing me about.

She knocked my glasses off. I tried to look for them, but could not see to find them. As I was very short-sighted, I was worried in case the lenses had been broken. Olga knew my dependency on my spectacles and was very angry and threatened the Polish girl with a small pen knife, which somehow she always had managed to keep, in order to cut and divide our group's ration of bread. The Polish girl did not argue any more and gave my spectacles back to me. Both my sister and I were much relieved to see that only the left side of the frame had been broken. I used a strip from my dress, which was getting shorter and shorter, to improvise a new left side to the spectacle frame, which I looped a few times about my ear.

WE HAD been travelling for a couple of hours when the SS guard mockingly ordered Tante Berthe, the eldest of our group, to sing a French song. Tante Berthe stood up as best she could in her weakened state and against the jolting movement of the train, and she tried to sing. But her voice was faint and she had forgotten the words. She started to tell the SS guard about her elegant past life in Paris. She told him: 'I was not dressed in rags as I am now, I wore beautiful, fine clothes. I went to the theatre, the concerts.....' We were very sad for Tante Berthe, for we never spoke of our past life among ourselves and certainly never to the SS. Our group was angry at the humiliation of Tante Berthe by the SS guard, but above all we were frightened for her, because we felt her mind might be slipping. At this point, Giuliana bravely said to the SS guard: 'I'll sing an Italian song.' The SS guard wanted Giuliana to sing again. She refused and said as if to herself in Italian, 'I did not sing for you.'

WE SPENT the rest of the day, the night and part of the fifth day, now the 22nd Jan 1945, travelling in the wagons. In the evening of the fifth day we were ordered off the train. The column of deportees was reformed by the SS and the death march resumed. At two o'clock in the morning of the sixth day 23rd Jan 1945 we arrived at Ravensbrück camp. We had to sleep outside on the snow. We lay close to each other, one blanket underneath two of us and one blanket covering us. It was bitterly cold and we could not stop shivering. When dawn came, we were marched to a reception area and given new numbers although we were not tattooed. My number was 99765, my sister had the next number. A large group of us were put in the washrooms and all the time we were in Ravensbrück camp, we had to sleep there on the bare floor, which was always covered with water. Our food ration was as bad as in Auschwitz-Birkenau and sometimes worse. The bread ration was smaller.

OLGA DEVELOPED bad stomatitis. Her gums were inflamed and ulcerated with running blood and pus. She was in so much pain, that I had to chew her hard bread ration and give it to her to swallow. That was the only way she could eat it.

WHILST WE were in Ravensbrück, there was a selection when I was separated from Olga. My number had not been taken and I was able to take advantage of an incident which disturbed the attention of the SS, and I rushed to rejoin my sister and take my chances with her. At that time we did not know the fate of either group. The SS sometimes changed tactics.

ON THE 11th Feb 1945, we were transferred to Malchow, north-east of Ravensbrück. We were put in a huge, single storey building with a concrete floor and windows. We slept on thin pallets. Our clothing was nothing but thin rags and was full of lice which caused a continuous itching. By now we were very much weaker. The bread ration had been getting smaller. Many deportees fainted at roll calls. We thought and spoke of nothing but food.

ON THE 2nd April 1945 we were transferred to Leipzig camp. There was no change in our small ration of food, nor in the brutal treatment of the SS towards us. In the evening of the 13th April, the SS evacuated the Leipzig camp. The only food we were given was our ration of bread for that evening. This second death march lasted nine nights and eight days during which we were given no food or drink, except once - a handful of raw rice. We kept a few grains in our mouth for a long time, to soften them before swallowing. We spent every night in the open, and we walked all day. We were in a terrible physical state. To get some moisture we chewed grass and spat it out, we ate dandelions and when we could get them, the tops of swedes. We had to be very careful for the SS shot anyone who went near the fields, stopped or lagged behind. Having survived the horrors of Auschwitz-Birkenau and the first death march, Tante Berthe, being older had weakened so much that she could no longer walk and she too was shot dead. We were devastated because she had kept up with us for so long. She had told us so many stories to keep up our morale. There were now only seven of our group of ten.

ON ONE occasion, when we passed a field of swedes, being nearest to the field, I stepped out of line to try and grab some swede tops. Olga pulled me back before I could reach the swede tops. As she pulled me back, we heard a rifle shot; the SS had been aiming at me. Throughout this second death march the number of rifle and revolver shots by the SS increased daily.

WE HEARD distant heavy gun fire. We hoped it was the Russian advancing from the East or the Allies from the West. The SS seemed to be in confused disarray and were marching us in circles. More than once we saw the same signposts.

ON THE 22nd April 1945 we finally arrived at the Elbe, at a small village which I remember as Lorenzkirch. We continued to hear heavy gunfire and we knew the battle was getting closer. During the whole day we saw German civilians crossing the Elbe over a small bridge, with their farm animals and horses and carts heavily laden with their belongings. They seemed to be evacuating because of the Russian advance. We deportees were taken to a field near the road within sight of the bridge. Rumours were that we were to wait until the German civilians had crossed the bridge, then our turn would come.

TWO OF our French friends whose names I cannot recall were now not with us. They may have trailed behind. We could find no news of them. I never saw them again. The remaining five of us, Giuliana Tedeschi, Julianne Hechter, Henriette, Olga and I happened to be on the edge of the field, close to the road. The SS guards still kept us in ranks of five. It was raining and cold and we were sitting on the wet grass. At dusk on the 22nd April, there was talk that the bridge had collapsed.

LATER WE heard men's voices speaking Italian coming from the road on the other side of a low wire fence. They were Italians who had been forced to work in Germany after Italy had been occupied by the Germans. We shouted to them and asked if they had any food. They only had a few raw potatoes to spare. We shared them amongst the five of us and ate them raw, peel and all to the amazement of the Italian men.

WE FELT that the SS were now becoming afraid themselves. The five of us took advantage of the dark night and decided to escape. We quickly crossed the road and carried on walking until we came to the back of a hut, where a group of Italians, in soldiers' uniforms, were actually boiling potatoes. They gave us some of the potatoes and sheltered us for the night. There must have been many deportees who had escaped, because in the morning of the 23rd April 1945, we could hear the SS shouting and threatening all escaped deportees to rejoin the column. The SS came so close to where we were, that the Italians quickly hid us under their long green-grey greatcoats. The five of us spent the rest of the day hiding, and before nightfall we found a wooden shed where we spent the night together with other deportees and Italians. Throughout the night we could hear the sound of gunfire. It was so close, we felt as if we were in the midst of it. At dawn on the 24th April there was a lull in the battle, and the five of us decided to go out and see what was happening.

AT SOME distance away, we saw a soldier mounted on horseback, coming towards us. To our great relief, it was a Russian officer, who on seeing our starved appearance, pointed to some suitcases on the side of the road, which contained some food left behind by the fleeing German civilians. On opening the suitcases which were full of all sorts of food, we took what we thought was bread, but was in fact a kind of meatloaf. Other deportees also came and helped themselves to the food; there was more than enough for all of us. The Russian officer, followed by his soldiers, made us understand that we should take the road in the opposite direction from the Elbe, towards the east. By then, many more deportees, women and men, were ahead and behind us. The road was through a thickly wooded area. On each side there were dead German and Russian soldiers, as well as dead horses. The battle had indeed been very close. About half way through the wooded area on the right-hand side of the road a French officer asked if there were any French deportees. Julianne Hechter and Henriette told him they were French. He said to follow him to the French camp. The five of us went in and we were given a hot meal. Then the French officer told Giuliana, Olga and me to rejoin the column of ex-deportees on the road, and make our way to Cottbus, about eighty kilometres from where we were. We embraced Julianne and Henriette and wished them a safe return home.

BY THIS time, Olga had developed a very painful and swollen knee. She had great difficulty in walking without my help. We rested several times. The two of us trailed behind the column. As we rested, I looked at her knee, and my thoughts went back to our sufferings in the camps and on the death marches and I knew that it was only the love that we always had for each other that gave us both the strength to survive.

WE COULD hear gunfire once again, and the Russian soldiers who passed us in the opposite direction made us understand that we must hurry, as there was a German counter attack. We finally came to the end of the wooded area where Giuliana was waiting for us. The three of us carried on walking until we came to a village which seemed deserted. Because we had trailed so far behind we could see no other ex-deportees. We were exhausted and Olga could walk no further. We entered one of the deserted houses, and slept on a bed for the first time in over twelve months. When we awoke the next morning we went outside and there was no one about, just the three of us. It was a strange and eerie feeling.

FROM THE 24th April 1945 to the 5th May 1945, the three of us walked from village to village, eating wherever we found food and sleeping in deserted houses. We washed ourselves and changed clothes and footwear wherever we could. We finally got rid of our lice. On one occasion, we entered the kitchen of a deserted house, where we found a huge saucepan, full of sauerkraut with potatoes and sausages, on the range and still warm. We helped ourselves, but suffered from diarrhoea for days. On another occasion, we saw some disbanded Italian soldiers who took us to a deserted farm and cooked us a meal.

ON THE 5th May 1945 after twelve days of walking, we reached Cottbus. The camp was run by the Russians for Assembly of Italian Military ex-internees, and was a large area of houses with a wired perimeter. We were the only three women there and we were allocated one of the houses. We were in Cottbus for seventy-six days and during the first five weeks we were terribly weak and ill with diarrhoea and sickness. There were no doctors or medicines. The Italian soldiers did what they could to help us. Slowly we were able to take some food and get a little stronger.

ON THE 15th July 1945, the whole camp left for Spremberg camp, also run by the Russians and similar to Cottbus. We stayed in Spremberg until the 2nd September 1945. I have an identity document signed by the Italian and Russian commandants to assist repatriation.

ON THE 2nd September 1945 the Russians took us all to a train, and we travelled in open wagons to Mittenwald on the Austrian border. The train stopped a few times each day and we were given food and drink. On the 9th September 1945, we arrived in Mittenwald, a camp run by the Americans and were greeted by being sprayed with DDT. Later we were given food and a place to sleep while we awaited our return journey to Milan.

CHAPTER FIVE

SURVIVAL

Life after Death

Photo: With my son David - 1948

THE NEXT morning, the 10th September 1945, we were taken to a train and we travelled in open wagons and arrived in Milan on the 12th September. We embraced Giuliana Tedeschi, who was to travel to Turin, said good-bye and wished for each other that our families would be safe at home.

AT A small office in Milan station, we were given an identity document. Mine is No. 59859. We were also given five thousand lire each. Olga and I were worried because we had no idea what had happened to our family. Our greatest fear was that our family members may have been deported. It was with great anxiety that I telephoned Giavanna Fogagnolo's bookshop where I had been arrested. I was very relieved to hear Miss Fogagnolo telling me that as far as she knew, the family was safe and living in Via Galvani School. Olga and I telephoned the school, who confirmed that our family was still there. We went to the school and found our father, step-mother and Rachel. As soon as we entered the schoolroom, Rachel ran towards us and we embraced. On seeing our father lying on his bed, we were very saddened at the deterioration in his health. He seemed to be overwhelmed by our return. Our step mother was crying.

It was a very emotional reunion. Our family had been very worried, because they did not know what had happened to Olga and me, after our arrests. Olga, a teacher of French and English, had been arrested near Ferrara in February 1944 by the Italian fascists. She was suspected of being a spy because her suitcase contained books in French and English. Later the Gestapo found she was Jewish and she was deported from Fossoli to Auschwitz-Birkenau in April 1944.

AT THE via Galvani School, my sister and I were given a camp bed and two blankets each. To accommodate us, the other camp beds had to be moved closer together. The room was full of men, women and children. There was no privacy at all. The school provided community meals. On the 29th September, 1945, all those living at the via Galvani School were transferred to via Monsivo School.

WHEN I felt stronger and before I was able to start work, I went to visit my friends of the Resistance who were with me in San Vittore prison, Miss Fogagnolo, Elena Banfi, Alba Zanfini and Renata Vico. Elena Banfi told me that Jim, the British prisoner of war, interpreter at San Vittore prison, was in Milan, working for U.N.W.R.A. I met Jim again at Elena Banfi's house, and he insisted that I go to A.P.P.I.A. and be registered as a member of the National Association for Persecuted Political Italian Antifascists. My membership number is 278 dated 1st November 1945.

OLGA WAS unable to find work in Milan and she accepted a Berlitz school of Languages post in Rome as a teacher of French and English. It was my intention to continue with my education, because I had always wanted to go to university to study medicine. But our financial circumstances were such that Rachel and I had to find employment. My father and step-mother were old and in poor health. On the 9th October 1945 Rachel and I found employment with the British Military, as interpreters/clerks.

ON THE 15th March 1946 we were transferred back to via Galvani School. My father had been unable to rent the flat in which we had lived before my arrest. I went to the Milan office of the British Military Town Major, who dealt with accommodation, to ask if he could help in arranging for my family to have private accommodation. I told him I was an Auschwitz survivor, now working for the British Military. In August 1946, we were allocated two rooms and a bathroom, part of a flat in via Caravaggio, on the fourth floor. From the balcony, I could see the cell windows of one of the six spars of San Vittore prison, where I was held as a political prisoner for six months, prior to my deportation to Auschwitz-Birkenau.

ON 26th September 1945, I returned to San Vittore prison to obtain certification of my detention there under the Nazi regime. I have a declaration signed by the Director which translates as follows:

"We declare that Miss Ancona Victoria, daughter of Saul, has been detained in this prison, from the 9th November 1943 to the 15th May 1944, at the disposal of the German SS, for political motives and for being Jewish, and from here sent to Fossoli.

The above as per register.
The Director."

ON THE day of our return to Milan, the 12th September 1945, the Centre for Assistance to Survivors from

Germany, allocated me 5,000 lire and on the 20th September 1945, 300 lire. On the 9th November 1945 I was given a dress and a pair of shoes. This was the last help I received. I expected to have a medical examination, but I was not given one. There was little Italian organisation to receive our train of survivors and certainly no Red Cross.

I FELT that survivors from the concentration camps needed professional help for them to accept that they had survived - when six million Jewish men, women and children had been murdered - to remove the guilt for having survived and to learn to live again. There was little help and virtually no understanding of our situation.

I RECEIVED no professional help and I had to rely on myself and the love of my family. I went about my day-to-day life, living it on the surface only, inside myself I was still in Birkenau and on the death marches. I felt I was still surrounded by an electric wire fence which I could not break through. The nights were worse. The nightmares were so clear and vivid, I was re-living the horrors of the concentration camps. I could not believe they were nightmares. I needed privacy and quietness to help me come to terms with life. I was pleased that Olga had settled in Rome and was living with a good and kind family whom she had known in Trieste.

AT THE end of March 1946, I met a British soldier, Alfred Vincent, who befriended me. Although I needed the help of a friend, I had not expected a man to show any interest in me. I learned later, that, on our first meeting he had seen the tattooed number on my left forearm, and he knew then that I had been in a concentration camp. He was gentle, kind and very patient. I began to look forward to being with him. With his help, I was gradually regaining my self-confidence.

IN AUGUST 1946, my family and I moved to the two rooms and bathroom allocated to us, and, shortly afterwards, Alfred and I became engaged. In December 1946 we were married, and in the summer of 1947 we came to Nottingham with our new son David.

I SETTLED into my life in England quite quickly. Having lived through nine years of terrible deprivation, the ration system in England seemed almost extravagant.

To my great surprise and delight, even sweets were on the ration card! I found Alfred's understanding a constant strength. And small things, such as friendly shopkeepers, willing and ready to be an encouragement as I adjusted to yet another new country, leave me with happy memories of my first years here.

SOON AFTER, in 1949, I began to suffer from headaches, which became progressively more violent and more frequent. I kept thinking of the terrible beatings on my head by the SS. In 1959, it was diagnosed that I was suffering from a condition, known as acromegaly. On the 15th February 1963, I underwent neurosurgery for the removal of a tumour and the pituitary gland (hypophsectomy). I do not know to what extent my illness was brought on by my experiences in the camp but in February 1963, the consultant neurosurgeon and consultant physician, stated in their letter to me that, "the onset of this illness was a few years after her release from concentration camp and it is very possible that the physical and mental stresses to which she was subjected in captivity were responsible for the development of acromegaly." Acromegaly causes enlargement of the bones and damage to the joints.

SINCE 1963 there has been very considerable deterioration in my general health. I have had bilateral total hip replacements, cervical spine disease and bilateral spastic paraparesis. My mobility is severely restricted. My eyesight became so poor, that I had to have lens implants in both eyes. In January 1991 it was necessary for me to have a permanent pacemaker for bradycardia.

FROM THE day we met my husband has been a constant source of strength to me. Throughout all my operations, illnesses and recurrent nightmares, my husband and son have lovingly nursed me, have taken care of me and have helped me to overcome many physical obstacles.

DAVID, OUR son, is married to Jill. We have a lovely granddaughter, Sarah Rachel Victoria and grandson Jonathan Alexander James.

OLGA NOW retired, continues to live in Rome. Her health is not good, but she shows the same determination to overcome her sufferings as she did when we were in the concentration camps. She still travels from Rome, each summer, to stay with Rachel and me. Rachel lives in Liverpool, and is now a widow. She has two sons, Albert and Gordon and two granddaughters, Jennifer and Fiona.

MY FATHER would have been very proud and happy to know that, after living through the racial laws against the Jews, living in hiding and surviving concentration camps and death marches, his three daughters are as close together today as they have always been.